the ARK Principle

A **Relevant, Capable,** and **Becoming Communication Strategy** for **Surviving** and **Thriving** in a **Turbulent World**

the ARK Principle

A **Relevant, Capable,** and **Becoming Communication Strategy** for **Surviving** and **Thriving** in a **Turbulent World**

angie stapleton

PALMETTO
P U B L I S H I N G
Charleston, SC
www.PalmettoPublishing.com

Hardcover ISBN: 979-8-8229-1165-9
Paperback ISBN: 979-8-8229-1166-6

dedications

Dad: your perfect example of what hard work, sacrifice, a "never give up" mindset, and selflessness actually look like are priceless gifts to me.

Mom: your perfect example of hard work and doing whatever it takes to make things happen, your sacrifice, your unrelenting support, and your selflessness are priceless gifts to me.

My husband (Big Angry): your gift of your story, time, support, and sacrifice are remarkable to me.
I am forever grateful.

acknowledgements

My two boys, Bradley and Clayton: my love for you both is indescribable. I am who I am in part because of you. Thank you for making me proud.

My sister: I would not be who I am without your unrelenting support. You are a bright shining light, and I love you dearly.

Kortnie: in part, it is because of your trust in me to help you communicate responsibly and assertively with colleagues that I had the epiphany of the ARK principle. Thank you. You are an amazing friend.

Blake: I am in part who I am because of your profound friendship. Thank you. You are an amazing friend.

contents

I am a licensed professional counselor for the State of Mississippi and currently employed at Mississippi Gulf Coast Community College. I am always on the lookout for proven motivational techniques to inspire others. Without any hesitation, I can say this is a must-read for anyone desiring to make the most of life.

"Beautiful," "smart," "fit," "hard-working," "friendly," "kind," "professional," "prepared," "confident," "ambitious," "popular," "dependable," "winning attitude," and "team player" are just some of the words that come to my mind when thinking about the author Angie Stapleton. Throughout her storied career, she has remained true to her values and upbringing and unfailingly committed to her students while in in her career. I first met Angie as an undergraduate student in 1984 at Faulkner State Community College. Angie was hand-selected by the college president to assist with recruitment. On one particular day as we worked together, and as it poured down rain, Angie had an umbrella; I did not. I said, "How did you know to bring an umbrella today?" Angie answered simply, "I watch the weather every morning; I am a farmer's daughter!"

At some point, I began to admire Angie's preparedness and intention. I understand that with a commitment, she also prepared for a vision to change lives with a specific strategy to communicate authentically. Angie used her personal experiences and wisdom as a farmer's daughter, as Miss Foley High, Miss Faulkner State, and Miss Alabama Agriculture, and her teaching experiences to forge improvement in the following areas: teaching her seventh-grade students to read at a tenth-grade level and developing and implementing a valuable tool to guide post-secondary students from matriculation to graduation. Her strategy and techniques further helped her define and develop the ARK Principle. In a time when our culture is complex, many people find themselves navigating through a myriad of obstacles. Now more than ever, it is necessary to consider innovative, creative ways to communicate that convey competence, resilience, and resourcefulness. Angie Stapleton's *The ARK Principle* offers this and much more. I wholeheartedly recommend this book.

Dr. Lisa Hammons, LPC-S,
Mississippi Gulf Coast Community College

preface

Calm, but alert. Relaxed, but ready.
Smooth, but sharp. Humble, but confident.

~ABPV

I was married, had two children, and had begun teaching when my attitude about communication changed. And I was forty-plus when I became aware that all my life, I had been complacent about communicating with intention and without negotiating who I am. I rarely ever thought about a specific strategy that would work in my favor until I assessed my past and present to reengineer a way to communicate with purpose and conviction. What I eventually realized was that I longed for a way to reason and negotiate that reflects logic *and* empathy. Many of my thoughts emanated from my emerging adulthood, motherhood, teaching and academic advising careers, and meeting my husband, all of which helped me sharpen my communication skills, quickly and aggressively. In a sense, those events all served as a crash course. Moving forward, once I fully evaluated my past lackluster approach, I became so stunned by my own incompetencies and by just how unintentional I had been in communicating that I decided to do something about it. Ultimately, I decided that I want to be a catalyst for a visionary way to lead positive communication. I also want to compound the success I have found with the ARK Principle strategy.

My fifth year as an academic adviser was a challenging year. Changes to my workplace and personal life were imminent by then. One day, a unique, challenging situation within the university transpired with my colleague, during which we reviewed effective ways to deliver a sensitive message. We struggled together with a few failed attempts. After some adjustments to the message to get results, the epiphany of the ARK Principle materialized in my mind. Once I shared the strategy with my colleague and she used it for the first time with success, I was encouraged. This inspiration came from a seemingly small moment yet propelled me toward some serious soul-searching. That moment eventually became the steppingstone of strength that moved me to what I believe to be a higher purpose. Trusting my intuition and intention at that moment forever changed my outlook on communication. It was also in that very moment I realized that, despite self-doubt and setbacks, I wanted to share what I discovered to be meaningful. I also realized I must trust my intuition enough to show others what is possible. At the very least, I decided that showing up and sharing what I discovered is important to me. Sharing the ARK Principle allowed me the opportunity to lean into the flow of my own happiness. That, I believe, is a gain.

In a sense, the ARK Principle is a warm recognition of my struggles and a thorough celebration of finding a comfortable place to communicate with just about anyone. The obstacles I feel I have had to overcome to manifest the ARK Principle have been painful, to say the least, but overcoming them has resulted in my wholeness. I have earnestly worked to turn my mess into a message, a message that I hope will translate into real world guidance that resonates with people around the world.

At some point, I knew I must deviate from unidimensional and mostly reactive communication because it was unpleasant and idle. Implementing the ARK Principle into my everyday life has helped me form stronger bonds and relationships to communicate tactfully, in an orderly way, and successfully. I continue to become increasingly aware of how powerful the ARK Principle actually is since it gives me a heightened sense of control. For those who feel as though communicating can be stressful, can cause untenable suffering, can be less than life-affirming, and can often be disorderly, there is hope. The ARK Principle holds the potential to prevent nonproductive communication and defuses nonproductive communication when it happens. The key is in the habit of communicating conscientiously and intentionally, with the ARK Principle components at the forefront. Though this strategy is not an absolute tool, my experience is that it is a formidable one.

Further, something that is incredibly important to me is to be a voice and force for people who feel painfully reserved and those who feel obtrusively energetic when communicating with others. Helping others discover these natural tendencies will help unlock important information regarding what level of balance is needed to use the ARK Principle. From there, focus and practice will make a way for adjustments, and adjustments will lead to improvement.

This book is a gift from my soul. I hope to dispense an organic way to help others maximize their communication potential through and with depth and honesty. The following chapters were developed out of communications and revelations from colleagues, business professionals, family, friends, and complete strangers, all of whom collectively helped me discover my potential. It is more than a story, then, and I share my thoughts with the people who stimulated the thoughts in the first place and anyone compelled to connect with what I have established as a result of these connections.

chapter 1

The **ARK** Principle

Conflict is inevitable, but combat is optional.

~Max Lucado

This book is an endeavor to bring *intention* to communication and to help others communicate in a way that is not only contributory and charitable, but also honest and straightforward. The ultimate goal of the ARK Principle is to achieve higher ground and to do that through focus and purpose. My hope is to recenter the way people communicate to achieve balance, stability, and poise. If being painfully reserved or obtrusively energetic is relatable, and even if some self-reflection is necessary to bring it to light, launching that awareness can be the spark that ignites the capacity for change. The growth in awareness may be unpleasant at times, but it is necessary to sustain essential relationships and to withstand nonessential ones.

The ARK (assertive, respectful, kind) Principle is a communication strategy and tool, one that that explores, articulates, and strategizes. This strategy has personally been transformative, and I believe it also has the power to revolutionize everyday communications for anyone seeking meaningful, influential ways to connect with others. It can be a stand-alone strategy and tool, but elaboration serves to provide clarity and to make the strategy more attainable. An in-depth exploration of the hallmark components, assertiveness, respectfulness, and kindness, reveals the importance of each and the connection among them. Considering all components and achieving a balance with them is essential to being successful with the strategy. The ultimate purpose of the ARK Principle is to advance social dexterity. Learning and applying this principle will, in turn, flex and advance social acumen.

I resisted for several years, not because I lacked the motivation, but because of the unknown. At some point, I decided it would all be OK. I would write this book because I am that passionate about the subject of clear, successful, powerful communication, communication that empowers and that earns and commands respect and honor. I would also write it because countless colleagues, business professionals, family, friends, and even others who don't know me that well have encouraged me to do so. In a sense, they have become passionate about me sharing the ARK Principle because they know it and use it with success. The rest, I hope, will take care of itself. So it has become my purpose and mission to advance others with my communication strategy, to help others develop the courage to speak the truth, and to evolve in such a way that future generations are strengthened.

The ARK Principle strategy is simple, yet how it manifested was complex. It is the result of a variety of factors, from my childhood, emerging adulthood, motherhood, teaching and academic professional career, and life itself. I've spent many years in unique environments and had extraordinary, unconventional experiences and education, both of which heavily influenced the way I communicate. Writing this book about the ARK Principle was an afterthought, meaning that when I created the principle, I had no intentions at the time to write a book about it. However, within a few years of investment, I found myself personally considering the ARK Principle both when I communicated and when I helped others communicate. And after being encouraged by everyone I share it with, I decided it was worth the effort to put something in writing about it. My hope is that it changes lives, one at a time. In fact, it has become a burden, a good burden, that is, to present this communication strategy for the benefit of anyone who is committed to minimizing social awkwardness, cooperating with the social platform of life, acknowledging there is an immense need for global shift because of the negative effect technology has had, and wanting to drive communications that positively affect the lives of other human beings.

In a community of unfettered access to numbing technology, many relationships have become superficial. Some even cease to exist. No matter what your path and history of communication has been in the past, I hope this strategy will change your mindset, if it needs that, to believe you have the power to transform your life and relationships with specific communication. Although results are crucial, it's not just about the results. The real magic is in the underlying power of the ARK Principle. This approach, as I use it, and others do too, stimulates attention and admiration when communicating. The ARK Principle is designed to teach individuals to focus on and trust in social skills by becoming a better listener, communicating with intention, and prioritizing empathy. It is also designed to equip people with communication tools that others perceive as competence and warmth. Persistence with the process of learning the skills will drive results. The reward is confidence and competence.

NOTE: To me, focus and trust are powerful. I consider this: trusting the ARK Principle to work, then putting it into practice, is akin to a personal experience of mine. My husband and I purchased a light twin Cessna aircraft for business (and personal) use, since we live in Gulf Shores, Alabama, and he professionally operates flights out of Houston, Texas. I spent the first two years thinking only about how uncomfortable I was in a small airplane. It was during that same timeframe that I came to terms with the fact that he had been flying since he was sixteen, had flown and later instructed flight in the US Navy, is currently a captain for a legacy carrier, and was simply born to fly. It's *who* he is. He felt so destined for flight that he worked as a newspaper boy to pay for flight lessons before he graduated high school. Regardless, it took time for me to adjust to the mindset that, with his aptitude and experience, for flying and maintenance, because he was professionally trained for both, if he couldn't mitigate any danger that arises, it was highly unlikely anyone else could either. I am happy to say that I fly with confidence now. What a gift; the views are amazing, and I would have totally missed out on that. Becoming confident with the ARK Principle felt similar. Developing, trusting, and implementing the strategy eventually led to accomplishment. Reaching the summit with it and "soaring" with it feels a lot like flying now.

At times I had doubt because few things in this world are absolute. But if there is something I am certain of, it is that if I fail to achieve something using the ARK Principle, it is not likely I would have been able to achieve it anyway. Communicating with confidence, ease, and effectiveness is a learned skill, and it is time-consuming, just like mitigating my thoughts about flying. Trust and focus lead to confidence, and confidence leads to competence. I trust this sequence.

The objective of the ARK Principle isn't perfection—or even excellence for that matter—but rather, some sense of competence with it. This takes time and effort, but it is worth it. Family and friends are worth it. Our contribution to society is worth it. Consider it one of the best investments ever made in the way of relationships and humanity. My experience is that the returns are likely priceless.

Why it works

The ARK Principle is a humanistic approach. Assertive: people *require* it. Respectful: people *deserve* it. Kind: people *need* it. It is the trifecta that is progressive, capable, and responsible. Developing the skill and attitude puts an emphasis on inner peace and contentment for which outward surroundings and circumstances are comparatively of less significance. It is about fostering an attitude that every communication opportunity requires a *specific* vantage point. It recognizes that every situation is a chance to become more capable of humane, cooperative, compassionate, realistic communication. And it champions the idea that a reliable strategy emphasizes both individual and social potential. It is the legacy of affirmation, ability, and responsibility. This is why I am so passionate about it.

Key Elements to the **ARK** Principle

"What you do makes a difference, and you have to be the one to decide what kind of difference you want to make."

~Jane Goodall

If there is one thing I have learned in life, it is that I need to advocate for myself. No one can do that like I can. Through my trials and triumphs, I have learned that this has made me more capable than I could have imagined and that it emanated from a focus on *offense* instead of *defense*. It is my ultimate aspiration to demonstrate to others how important it is to self-advocate and to stand firm in order to gain proper authority in conveying everyday messages. It is equally important to me to demonstrate a strategy that is accessible, tangible, and replicable.

At some point, too, I remember becoming hopelessly drawn to reading. I also decided that if I was going to read, I was also going to invest in myself. I put myself on a path to self-improvement, recreationally reading every book and listening to every podcast that supported that cause. Something I noticed, though, was that what I read and listened to did not give me a specific strategy to implement all the advice I wanted so desperately to follow. It was this "I see it,

I hear it, I feel it, but how do I *do* it?" ongoing conversation I had with myself. It was this component that ultimately led me to focusing on a specific *strategy* for everything I wanted to implement. Regardless, all the books and podcasts I had explored had changed my life so positively that I eventually committed to writing my own book for others. More specifically, this self-improvement is directed at communication, for me and others, specifically through the refinement of soft skills. This book is a hybrid of many books and podcasts that changed my outlook on life, relationships, and communication. The information that I share came from a great need. I hope that what I have learned will help others discover the power to advocate for themselves through carefully considered, purposeful communication.

Almost every book and podcast I have explored has changed my life one increment at a time. Some are self-help, and some simply touched my soul in some form or another, even if it was not specifically self-help. Two books in particular inspired me to read and explore more, which eventually created an awareness in me for which I am ever so grateful. *Outliers: The Story of Success,* by Malcolm Gladwell, is perhaps one of the most noteworthy, as it brims with accessible, attractive ideas that are backed by respected research. This is where I learned that IQ has a threshold, meaning once a certain threshold in intelligence is reached, "the points do not translate into any measurable real-world advantage." [1] Further study indicates it is clear that IQ is only one factor that contributes to effectiveness and success.

EQ, emotional quotient (otherwise known as EI, emotional intelligence), or practical intelligence, (e.g., self-awareness, impulse control, persistence, zeal, self-motivation, and empathy) is the ability to recognize, understand, and manage emotions within ourselves and with others. The extent to which this ability is considered and engaged alters our everyday interactions. In Chapter 4 of Gladwell's *Outliers: The Story of Success*, he explains further:

"The skill that Robert Sternberg calls 'practical intelligence' is knowing what to say to whom, when to say it, and how to say it for maximum effect. It is procedural: it is about knowing *how* to do something without necessarily knowing why you know it or being able to explain it. It's practical in nature: that is, it's not knowledge for its own sake. It's knowledge that helps you read situations correctly and get what you want. And, critically, it is a kind of intelligence separate from the sort of analytical ability measured by IQ. To use the technical term, general intelligence and practical intelligence are "orthogonal": the presence of one doesn't imply the presence of the other".[2]

Gladwell's book piqued my curiosity about emotional intelligence and its effect on life. From there, it sparked another curiosity about what drives success and happiness on a more personal level. Later I discovered *Emotional Intelligence: Why It Can Matter More Than IQ*, by Daniel Goleman. I learned in this book too that there is a crucial set of distinct abilities that matter in life, ones that distinguish excellence in real life. These abilities foster character, self-discipline, and compassion, which in turn, foster reliable, worthwhile relationships, personally and professionally. Goleman argues that all those abilities are considered to be the ones needed to thrive. The neurological and behavioral research that Goleman addresses in *Emotional Intelligence: Why It Can Matter More Than IQ* not only was life-changing for me, but also confirmed that emotional intelligence is "both distinct from academic abilities and a key part of what makes people do well in the practicalities of life." [3] Goleman describes qualities that help people excel in life, help relationships flourish, help one read another's innermost feelings, help rein in emotional impulse, and help one perform in such a way that others take notice.

Also compelling is that although IQ is relatively a fixed number at birth, emotional intelligence is a set of learned skills that when nurtured and strengthened have immense potential to transform and elevate communication. These, as Goleman describes, are the capacities required for living in social harmony. Based on Goleman's book, it is evident that understanding the emotional architecture of the brain and its correlation to communication is paramount for efficacy when communicating. In Goleman's introduction to his book, he writes: "In the Nicomachean Ethics, Aristotle's philosophical enquiry into virtue, character, and the good life, his challenge is to manage our emotional life with intelligence. Our passions, when well exercised, have wisdom; they guide our thinking, our values, our survival. But they can easily go awry, and do so all too often. As Aristotle saw, the problem is not with emotionality, but with the appropriateness of emotion and its expression." [4]

To say that this information heavily influenced the way I communicate and interact is an understatement. Over the years, I have used this knowledge to achieve many goals, many of which may not have been possible without the message. What I write about in this book is an extension of what I learned along the way in an effort to help others achieve the same satisfaction.

Important to mention is that aiming at a goal, whether it is a better job or better communication, radically increases the probability of achieving it. Taking that aim, directing that aim, and practicing it is worthwhile. Though easier said than done, an intentional aim with the right pressure gets results.

In another vein, but important to mention, is that although it is impossible to control what is happening or what others say and do, it is useful to consider *proactive*, powerful communication that minimizes potentially harmful reactive responses. My belief is that this is useful. My whole life changed when I realized that humility and calmness alongside assertiveness could coexist with difficult circumstances and conversations. The goal is just not to tolerate inappropriate behavior and disrespect. I concluded that it is important for self-preservation, the preservation of others beyond that, and the preservation of the entire communication platform, wherever it is, with whomever.

Composure

Likely one of the most influential, powerful words in my vocabulary as a result of discovering the ARK Principle is *composure*. It is likely the single most important piece to the ARK Principle. Its value is its effect on success, survival, and well-being. It has nothing to do with giving up dignity, respect, or control, but rather it is about maintaining poise, self-assurance, and presence of mind.

In order to navigate rough waters of communication, self-command is paramount. I believe that once composure is lost, the mind shifts dramatically to negative space. Composure is essential, and it demonstrates decisiveness. It is a calmness or repose of the mind, bearing, and appearance, meaning that it is applicable to words and actions. Becoming acquainted with, grasping for, and demonstrating mastery of composure will most certainly directly affect mastery of the ARK Principle. This is a noteworthy place to start. Adopt the responsibility and notice the change. Harness it. In an improved state, it will be a trustworthy guiding force.

Strategy

Likely one of the most used words in my career as a post-secondary academic adviser was *strategy*; as a result, and to this day, I have a healthy respect for strategy in most platforms. Strategy (approach) is necessary for staying the course and reaching a goal. Though many of my adult students were not first-time students, online education was a new experience for them. The best thing I could do for my students, then, was work with them to develop the right strategy for success. It involved my intuitiveness, my expertise in my field, my reliance on healthy communication, and the students' hard work and reliance on me to pull everything together. (It's important to mention that I heavily considered soft skills to be as important as hard skills, for both my students and me.) My record demonstrated success with strategy at the forefront. I believe it was because of the thoughtful plan I devised to assist students, one course at a time, to graduate. Looking back on this professional experience, it is also at this point the idea of strategy became much more significant because of necessity. Fortunately, and eventually, it led me to carefully developing a specific strategy for other platforms, namely communication. Ultimately, this was the catalyst for the ARK Principle.

Control

The "circle" of control is limited. Focusing on what is realistically "within" one's control is conducive to efficient communication, and identifying what the components are also provides clarification and deserves emphasis: my effort, words, actions, emotions, self-care, thoughts, and how others are treated. Effort, words, actions, emotions, self-care, thoughts, and consideration for others is "within" our control and conscientiously believing in their relevance serves as a fulcrum for comprehensive, fair communication.

Universally, I have determined that nearly every individual with whom I have connected agrees that better, more effective communication is a highly desirable tool for life. Communication is at the epicenter of every meaningful, productive relationship. Happiness and contentment in life are influenced by that. Yet, more times than not, those relationships suffer because of unintended communication errors. Whether the relationship is with children, parents, siblings, spouses, colleagues, or a perfect stranger, there is room for improvement.

I also believe that everyone has the capacity to lead and influence positively. Leading is not dominating; it is an art of persuading people to envision a common goal. Adopting and adapting to that individual mindset to communicate will drive success. So then the question is, How is success measured? It is my belief that the quality of relationships and the communication in them can precipitate success. Here is what I trust: confidence fits every lifestyle. Embrace confidence and employ the proper strategy to communicate, and the results will transpire. The caliber and integrity of my communication skills are substantially better than what they used to be. I feel and see that, and it is valuable.

chapter 3

Assertive

*"To be passive is to let others decide for you.
To be aggressive is to decide for others.
To be assertive is to decide for yourself...and to
trust that there is enough and you are enough."*

~Edith Eva Eger

Developing the skill of being assertive while remaining in control (i.e., respectful and kind at the same time) is paramount to success; at least that is my interpretation. Assertiveness can serve as a driving force for safe, healthy, meaningful communications for tougher-than-average messages, even ones that may seem innocuous. It is best used proactively. However, even if used reactively, the same principle applies. Most importantly, assertiveness is not simply the mere absence of passiveness or aggressiveness. It is, most times, the willingness to announce a want or need and/or express a viewpoint in a diplomatic way.

The magical combination is when assertiveness is complemented by respectfulness and kindness. This synergy will serve to drive communications that help others understand and relate to what the central message is, which is being firm yet highly reasonable, building trust, ensuring dignified communication, and therefore, strengthening relationships.

Using the ARK Principle will ultimately be the strategy for relevant, purposeful communication that, once mastered, will create intention. Results may or may not be visible right away; however, consistency with it will drive the results. There will be times of limited progress or regression, but this need not be a deterrent. The truth remains: consistency generates energy, and persistence and insistence fuel that energy. It is possible to recover from ineffective communication techniques. If the desire exists, so does the potential for change, first adequately, then extensively.

Examining a detailed description of assertiveness is beneficial and will further lead to expressive use of it. Being assertive is achieving a balance between aggressive and passive. Some points to consider are that assertion is bold, firm, decisive, simple, and direct. It is not high pressure or combative, like aggression. Assertiveness is distinctive, ambitious, and powerful. Achieving this balance stabilizes emotions so they are controlled enough to communicate in a way that is accurate and fitting for the circumstances. Without assertiveness, one's emotions gravitate to either end of the spectrum; that is, either aggressiveness or passiveness emerges. Being assertive is also *selfless*. It is also considered to be a more neutral position because implementation of it conveys that others' thoughts are of equal significance.

Assertiveness requires careful listening without interruption, clearly stating needs, wants, and facts, using appropriate tone, volume, and cadence and exhibiting positive body language. It is also a gift to all who attain it, most effectively when used in conjunction with respectfulness (manners plus responsibility) and kindness (charity plus humility). When achieved, it provides a safe environment to actively enable distinctive communication.

Below are five steps to learn assertive communication:[5]

1. Be factual about what you don't like.
   "We were supposed to meet at 11:30, but now it's 11:50." *instead of* "You're so rude! You are always late."

2. Don't judge or exaggerate.
   "Now I have less time to spend at lunch because I need to be back to work by 1:00." *instead of* "Now lunch is ruined because you were late."

3. Use "I" messages; "you" messages appear judgmental. Although clear, concerned, and concise messages that are void of defensiveness will not alone resolve a conflict, they are less likely to provoke hostility.

4. "I feel disrespected when you are not punctual for work." *instead of* "You are rude and disrespectful because you are late all the time."

5. Put it all together; use factual statements rather than judgmental ones. The formula is: "When you (their behavior), I feel (your feelings)."
   "<u>When you</u> **yell**, <u>I feel</u> **attacked**."

6. List behavior, results, and feelings. The formula is: "When you (their behavior), then (the results of their behavior), and I feel (how you feel).
   "<u>When you</u> **arrive late**, **I have to wait**, and <u>I feel</u> **frustrated and disrespected**."

I have also trusted Dr. Daniel Amen's insight in his book *Magnificent Mind at Any Age* in Chapter 15, "Brain Trust: Enhance Your Social Networks." Some additional thoughts from Dr. Amen's book provide important points to consider about assertiveness and how to achieve it:

"It's very important to say what you mean. Assertiveness and communication go hand in hand. Assertiveness means you express your thoughts and feelings in a firm yet reasonable way, not allowing others to emotionally run over you and not saying yes when it's not what you mean." Do not equate assertiveness with becoming mean or aggressive.

Here are five rules for achieving assertiveness:[6]

1. Do not give in to the anger of others just because it makes you uncomfortable.

2. Do not allow the opinion of others to control how you feel.

3. Say what you mean and defend what you believe is right.

4. Maintain self-control.

5. Be kind, if possible.

When we assert ourselves in a firm yet kind way, others have more respect for us and they treat us accordingly. If you've allowed others to mistreat you for a long time, they're going to be resistant to change. If you are persistent, you help them learn a new way of relating to you, and the relationship will likely improve. Ultimately, the by-product is heightened self-respect.[7]

It is my experience that fostering assertiveness in an effort to gain insight into options and alternatives when communicating contributes to improved performance. It is also my experience that assertiveness develops the ability within us to send and receive messages in a consistent and reliable way.

chapter 4

Respectful

"For to be free is not merely to cast off one's
chains, but to live in a way that respects
and enhances the freedom of others."

~Nelson Mandela

Assuming the best in difficult situations can easily be achieved with a considerate, gracious attitude to back it up. Respectfulness earns admiration, attentiveness, and regard, and that is how trust is built best. The effect of respectfulness is that it drives engagement, resilience, and satisfaction, the forces with which to communicate in demanding and challenging situations. Crossing the boundary into an area where respectfulness does not exist will eventually create an environment for inappropriateness and clusters of inefficiencies in communications. Using "please" and "thank you" and other supportive words proves to be uplifting. Though these seemingly plain words appear to be oversimplified, they are effective.

Being respectful also means that tone and volume should be heavily considered. Condescending words, tone, or body language perpetuates not being able to get to the heart of the matter; plus, disrespectful language and tone show lack of regard, control, and responsibility. This disrespectfulness will eventually dismantle trust and likely lead to further erosion of relationships. Body language (more on this topic in Chapter 9) and words alike must be polite and positive—when they are, they will be of great value.

Respectfulness includes listening to and understanding others' points of view. It is about compromise and consideration. Plus, it builds safety, trust, and openness. Considering alternative and more creative ways to address concerns within a conversation is particularly useful. Important to mention is that assuming the very best of the person you are speaking to, at least in tone, words, and body language, is a significant way to improve your position as a communicator.

In Jordan Peterson's 1*2 Rules for Life: An Antidote to Chaos*, Rule 9, "Assume That the Person You Are Listening to Might Know Something You Don't," he makes a relevant point:

"The final type of conversation, akin to listening, is a form of mutual exploration. It requires reciprocity on the part of those listening and speaking. It allows all participants to express and organize their thoughts…This kind of conversation constitutes active philosophy, the highest form of thought, and the best preparation for proper living…stable enough to be secure, but flexible enough to transform… Assume that the person you are listening to might know something you don't." [8]

Respectful communication also has hallmark qualities. Focusing on these qualities will engender trust and leave way for authentic, open, purposeful communication.[9]

1. *Nourish*: Needs are fulfilled.

2. *Autonomy*: Right of choice is foundational to being respected as a unique individual.

3. *Reciprocity*: Consider others; it requires mutuality and equality (everyone matters).

4. *Empower*: Contribute to others.

5. *Embrace*: Embrace differences and see the value in that.

Respectfulness is an essential component. From there, boundaries can be established, and areas of compromise can be too.

chapter 5

Kind

"Human kindness has never weakened stamina or softened the fiber of a free people. A nation does not have to be cruel to be tough."

~Franklin D. Roosevelt

Kindness, in most cases, demonstrates some presence of humility. I believe it is only fitting that because kindness is universally appreciated, it is useful to contemplate the power of kindness and humility when communicating in difficult situations, whether they are with demanding individuals or not. Though kindness seems generic, it is anything but that. It is gentleness, selflessness, and thoughtfulness. The depth to which we tap into potential with communication has potential to determine the direction in which it flows.

Kindness is the "binder," or cohesive component, that makes the ARK Principle uniting. When I encounter kindness in someone, whether personally or professionally, it becomes a foundation for more proper communications. Kindness has the potential to minimize deleterious effects of improper words and actions and therefore warrants more consideration. A modest view of one's own importance is the hallmark of anyone truly seeking to engage in quality, high-caliber communication. It is elevating and liberating to say the least.

Being kind requires thought and intention. And unexpected kindness is a grand intention, it matters, and it is applicable in more situations than not. The quote from Aesop sums it up. "No act of kindness, no matter how small, is ever wasted."

Research on kindness puts perspective on its importance. An article in Psychology Today titled "The Science of Kindness 101," by Dr. David Fryburg, is reflective of that. Dr. Fryburg is a physician and co-founder of a nonprofit organization, Envision Kindness. As he worked on Envision Kindness with his son, he became increasingly curious about the biology and psychology of kindness. Here is what he found:

"Wow—it became really clear that kindness wasn't just a nice and moral quality. It was baked into our biology. You can see it in toddlers and in many species of animals, including insects. It is a key to survival of a species. And when I learned that people who volunteered regularly had death rates 20-40 percent lower than those who do not, I was floored.

"People's mental and physical health are strongly benefited by kindness. All this biology meant that people's mental AND physical health were strongly benefited by kindness and that kindness isn't just a 'nice or moral' thing to do, but it is as influential to their health is clean water or vaccinations. This is huge."[10]

Although kindness is just one component to consider when communicating, it is an influential one. My experience is that kindness accomplishes way more than force ever could.

chapter 6

A Deeper Understanding of the ARK Principle

"The noblest pleasure is the joy of understanding."

~Leonardo da Vinci

I believe assertive, respectful, and kind to be the magical combination for empowering people to communicate on a level that achieves positive results, manages positive interactions, *and* provides a foundation for change. It permits powerful communication to take place, allows for leadership qualities to emerge, and promotes the capacity for productive, pragmatic, and constructive personal development.

Achieving Assertiveness

There is an art to being assertive and mindful with communications, versus being aggressive or passive. So what is the real difference and why is it so important? This part of the ARK Principle is paramount to success with it, and once this part is mastered, the other two parts of the principle seem to dutifully follow.

Assertive is not inciting. It will not likely drive negativity, but rather, it is thought-provoking and inspiring. The goal with assertiveness is to create a platform for growth, minus any negativity. Assertiveness will create resistance, but in a positive light, if properly used. This is essential. It is akin to the balance on a tight rope. In fact, learning assertiveness is best described as a tight rope walk. Leaning too far to the left or right will cause an imbalance, and at some point, a *falling* and *failing* point.

Aggressive, on the other hand, is overambitious, combative, self-seeking, and high-pressured. Sometimes, aggressiveness even involves physical contact or verbal attack. Though aggressive treatment and communication are required in severe or emergency situations and are considered acceptable in professional arenas such as the military, aggression usually does not work to drive positive, effective communication in the rest of the world. In fact, it is usually counterproductive, and at times, it precipitates danger. For many people, this will collapse emotions and prevent further communication. More importantly, this type of communication not only is ineffective, but also does long-term damage.

Because this piece of the ARK Principle is so powerful, I have included a chart below that I found at the Berkeley Well-Being Institute. It is a glimpse of differentiations among passive, assertive, and aggressive behavior:

Passive	Assertive	Aggressive
Too scared to say what you think	Expresses self clearly and confidently	Expresses self with aggression and irritation/anger
Avoids eye contact	Maintains eye contact	Stares in a judgemental way

Passive	Assertive	Aggressive
Speaks softly or weakly	Speaks firmly	Speaks loudly (e.g., shouting)
Reduces own self-esteem	Increases own self-esteem	Reduces others' self-esteem
Makes body smaller (e.g., slouching)	Firm yet welcoming posture	Closed posture (e.g., making body bigger)
Others' needs are put first	Self and others' needs are taken into account	Own needs are put first
Can't say 'no' to others' requests or demands	Is able to say no in a calm and direct way	Says no in an aggressive and reactive way
Aims to please others	Aims to express needs	Aims to win

Figure 1-1 (passive, assertive, aggressive) [11]

Assertive

To develop the skill of being assertive, consider and practice these seven principles:

1. Keep communication simple, specific, direct, and concise.

2. Keep communication aimed at understanding, instead of reacting/speaking quickly.

3. Don't raise your voice; rather, focus on the message.

4. Use positive body language (e.g., stand tall; put your shoulders back; make good eye contact; use a confident, calm, meaningful tone whether in person, on the phone, writing an email, or otherwise communicating)

5. Focus on the facts.

6. Remove unnecessary and harmful emotions.

7. Stay calm and poised.

Respectful

Though it might seem contradictory to be assertive and respectful at the same time, the two are more synonymous than not. Respectfulness requires deep consideration and regard. It also requires attentiveness, politeness, and reverence. When used with assertiveness, respectfulness provides a feeling of admiration. To develop the skill of being respectful, consider and practice these seven principles:

1. Keep communication polite and positive.

2. Keep communication aimed at behaving in a way that creates confidence in the audience even if it is one person.

3. Listen with intent *and* to understand.

4. Address communication with responsibility.

5. Communicate based on what is right, not who you like.

6. Be thoughtful of what and with whom you are communicating.

7. Be present.

Kind

Though it might feel as though this is covered with assertiveness and respectfulness, there is a little more. Consider and practice these seven principles:

1. Be generous and considerate.

2. Be friendly.

3. Be empathetic.

4. Be supportive.

5. Be courteous.

6. Be gentle.

7. Move communication forward with decency, humility, and generosity.

The first awareness: aggressive vs. passive

Acknowledging the space you occupy, meaning establishing awareness of aggressive or passive tendencies, is important. My experiences over time reveal that most individuals are one or the other. For many people, identifying this component and desiring to change it will be the infrastructure to establish the use of the ARK Principle.

The first part of establishing successful communication is to determine whether you need to *tone it down* or *toughen up*. Establishing that first will serve as a platform for creating palatable communications in difficult situations, regardless of the platform or audience. If your tendency is to be aggressive, the goal is to consider ways to become more humble and approachable. If your tendency is to be passive, the goal is to consider ways to become bolder and more capable. The goal is to be assertive, not aggressive or passive, to be confident, bold, and decisive, none of which is self-serving. Develop a repertoire of words, actions, and attitudes that exemplify what that is. Personalities can influence this all, which makes it relative to a certain point. However, with careful consideration, it is not impossible to account for definitive ways to be assertive, confident, bold, and decisive while remaining respectful, kind, and humble, which are regarded by the vast majority to be just that.

The second awareness: overcoming aggressiveness and passiveness

Practice daily to overcome the obstacles causing the aggressiveness or passiveness; different techniques work for different individuals because we are all unique. Rehearsing words and phrases out loud that exemplify *assertiveness* usually proves to be successful. Role-play, listen to podcasts, read, stand in front of the mirror, or simply rehearse these mentally.

Further, consider consulting with a person whom you respect and value. For me, this is my sister. She is a deputy program manager for a major tech company. Without a doubt, no matter what situation I face, I know she never fails to provide a diplomatic, comprehensive, resourceful plan to dispatch a critical message. Her job depends on it, and I depend on her. It was through my own quest *and* her valuable guidance that I developed and learned confidence with the ARK Principle.

Aggressive behavior and words are self-serving, and at times, they appear militant. This disposition implies a noticeable dominance and disregard of others. In an emergency or other dire situation, aggression can be appropriate and fitting. In fact, anything else is counterproductive. However, for everyday communications, aggression is likely to cause a reasonable person to feel unsafe and insecure. It also has the potential to bring out the worst in others. It is antagonistic, intrusive, and threatening. I have concluded that most individuals, unless they are in the military or in an arena that requires more aggressive approaches, do not respond positively to aggression. Conversely, passive behavior and words often involve retreating, saying and doing nothing at all. There is potential for others to violate personal rights regarding respect and dignity.

Vulnerability is important. Important to remember is that vulnerability does not equate to weakness. Instead, it is the willingness to try, to be consistent while trying, and to trust the environment enough to keep trying. Being vulnerable is difficult and is not typical or natural for most; however, when others convey vulnerability, it is estimated to be favorable. Potentially this awareness will be useful in determining what level of vulnerability will be considered helpful.

Vulnerable is a word that can be viewed as having a negative or positive connotation, and if examined, both are represented. In relation to the ARK Principle, what is referenced is the positive connotation, of course. In this sense, vulnerable means accessible (reachable, approachable, welcoming) and courageous (brave, confident). Being vulnerable fosters good mental and emotional health, because from it comes the ability to confront emotions more easily, as opposed to suppressing them. What evolves from that is the capacity to be more resilient and brave, while embracing our authentic self. This, in itself, changes the complexion of communication.

Developing a climate of vulnerability, enough to create a capacity for change, and not so much as to create chaos, is akin to the tightrope walking of *aggressive vs. assertive.* Being perceptive about what the situation requires is essential. It is also crucial to be aware that some situations and interactions will require more vulnerability than others. Using *intuitiveness* will be necessary in determining the proper level of vulnerability that is required to make gains in communication.

chapter 7

The Proactive Approach

"If you're proactive, you focus on preparing. If you're reactive, you focus on repairing.

~John C. Maxwell

The focus of this approach is to assess and implement strategies that promote awareness of words, phrases, and body language for proactive communication. This kind of communication exemplifies self-command, empathy, and consideration, but it is not authoritative or overly ambitious. The emphasis is on *anticipating* future challenges and preparing to overcome them with a semblance of control. *The "reacting" is done ahead of time.*

1. **Deliberately focus on ways to be more capable.**

   Contemplate ways to improve communications by remembering conversations that could or should have been different. Identify specific words, phrases, and gestures that require change. Find alternatives and begin implementing them.

2. **Set realistic goals to achieve productive communication.**

   Contemplate strategies to improve communication and execute them when the motivation surfaces. Journal areas of improvement, and make note of progress as it occurs. Don't be too hard on yourself; practice will facilitate improvement.

3. **Develop foresight to communicate clearly and assertively.**

   Role-play if necessary for this one; this step is essential to being somewhat prepared for a conversation, at least on some level. Prioritizing quality of words and body language over quantity of words and body language will get the job done.

4. **Prevent unwanted, unproductive communication.**

   Stand your ground. It is essential to act in a way that exudes confidence yet is mindful, defines the truth, and aims at achieving a certain goal with the communication. When delivering a message, remain consistent, firm, and fair.

5. **Invent ways to create desired communications.**

   Come up with unique ideas regarding how to implement the ARK principle. Because there are so many factors that can outline what feels comfortable, find a rhythm.

Learn *and* comprehend ways to tailor your conversations to align with the ARK Principle. When these are established and used successfully, put them in your back pocket.

chapter 8

The Reactive Approach

"...less impulsive, less reactive, more creative, and more centered."

~Deepak Chopra

The focus of this approach is to assess and implement strategies that promote the awareness of words, phrases, and body language for *reactive* communication. Reactive thinking is connected to the thought that stimulus and response are linked, and there is a recognizable gap between the two. The gap, and the knowledge surrounding it, wherein lies the ability to perceive, feel, and be conscious of a stimulus, means that stimulus need *not* solicit a certain response. Considering that gap is the key.

1. **Deliberately focus on ways and reasons miscommunication has occurred.**
    In considering what factors contributed to miscommunication, more serviceable deliveries can be contemplated and considered. Think about what went wrong and why, and consider valuable, meaningful ways to improve

upon that. Journal if necessary so there is an account of the events to study from in order to prevent a repeat version. Research or reach out to a trusted, respected friend or family member. Giving thought to others' perspectives is beneficial in gaining insight.

2. **Set realistic goals and a path for improvement with miscommunication.**

   Investigate reasons why miscommunication occurred. Look for loopholes. Many times, it can be traced and identified as something that could have been said differently, simply because emotions were out of line or facts were misrepresented. Take the time to find out what it is and how that can be modified. Set a goal or devise a plan that is realistic yet challenging. This will provide clarity for future communications.

3. **Develop the foresight to react in a way that shows responsibility and care.**

   Be patient and understanding when communications do not go as planned. Develop the ability to predict outcomes. (Future behavior can be predicted by reviewing past behavior.) Although the prediction might not be 100 percent accurate, it is useful to build on past experience to contemplate better ways to deliver a message. For first-time communications, revert to the ARK Principle.

4. React to unproductive communication with dignity.

When communications don't go as planned, resolve to react in a way that does not cause more damage. Use restraint until you have time to think through the communication without bias and until there is time to consider and evaluate future positive communications, if possible. If the conversation must go on, be diplomatic and controlled. Words gone bad leave a lasting bad impression. Time can usually bring about resolution because time gives you space to think.

5. Create a positive environment for future communications.

Never underestimate the power of a positive environment, one in which there is trust, cooperation, accountability, and equity. This environment is comfortable, though it may not be ideal or perfect.

chapter 9

Psychology in Communication

"The most important thing in communication is hearing what isn't said."

~Peter Drucker

Communication is not just about an exchange of words. It is more complex than that. Therefore, it is important to consider gestures, mannerisms, and expressions as part of the communication equation. Nonverbal communication, referred to as body language, is a crucial component. It has the capacity to develop in us comfort, likeability, and dignity, without any words spoken.

Research indicates that 60–90 percent of communication is nonverbal.[12] This is substantial, which means it is worth creating an awareness about it. Evaluating the effects of body language and the psychology behind it will support understanding it and using it to improve overall communication.

"Positive body language helps the person be more assertive and assists in putting their opinion forward. Positive body language is liked by others, and the person showing positive body language gets more attention and favor in any discussion." [13]

Positive body language includes posture (straight, yet relaxed and flexible), space (slight distance when sitting or standing), leaning (with intention, but without drawing attention), eye contact (frequent enough to show engagement and at a comfortable level), and affirmative movements (smiling and hand gestures to show engagement and increase likeability).

Becoming wise about how body language affects communication has been transformational for me. My post-secondary studies in psychology influenced this, but it mostly derived from my zeal for important ways to communicate more efficiently. I remember a TEDx talk I watched many years ago, when I was teaching middle school students. I frequently drew on my psychology background to assist me in guiding teenagers with teenager "matters," specifically with self-confidence and assertiveness. This TEDx video not only framed the way I helped young people navigate their difficulties, but also ultimately became an important component to developing pertinent details for using the ARK Principle. The TEDx talk is by Ann Washburn, a former engineer in flight simulation and explosives professional turned communication and body language expert. Her experiences with communication, quite like I remember mine before a positive focus, were lackluster. As a result, she also felt an overwhelming distance between her and the world. In an effort to improve her life, she began studying body language and changed her life.

In this video, Ann Washburn explains what she learned first, that is, how important it is that "updates" are made to previous subconscious programming, quite like computer programs. Since our brains daily process over forty million pieces of information every second, the updates create efficiency. Moreover, it can be problematic when we fail to make the necessary updates. Making some adjustments periodically, therefore, has potential to make us more conscientious, present, and efficient.[14]

In making updates to her subconscious to create efficiency in communication, Ann Washburn reflected on her body language and the negative effect she felt personally. In her reflections and accommodations, she discovered that her own body language required some fine-tuning. What she also learned from gaining expertise in the area of body language is that our subconscious mind operates body language. Since the subconscious is working on "programs," it makes sense to tune the "programs." An equally vital part of what she learned is in reference to speech, tone, and gestures (body language): when speech, tone, and gestures are not complementary, people will believe the *gestures* they see.[15]

Ann Washburn changed her life, and now changes others' lives, with the awareness that at times we fail to communicate authentically and accurately, simply because our minds require calibration to improve upon thoughts and gestures. At the end of the TEDx talk, she shares a poignant story, which is the main reason I share this piece. Her story is about her son, who was thirteen at the time. After moving four times and changing schools that many times, he struggled with making friends. At that time, too, Ann felt as though her son began to notice a change in her. Upon arriving home from his first day at his fourth school, he approached his mom about some potential reasons why his peers were dismissive. She delivered, and he listened to, a seemingly simple message about changing the way he stands. She only explained to him that standing with weight on both feet and keeping his hands by his side unless using them to convey a message was body language that conveys strength. Two weeks went by before any other exchanges were made about the conversation, until one day, Ann's son returned home from school with an obvious, different attitude. Ann knew her son had something important to share, so she waited patiently. After a few minutes, he confessed that her advice worked! (It is my belief that any mom will take that "win" any day from an adolescent!) He had made some friends and had adjusted to the new school. At the end of the year, Ann gave him the option to change schools. His reply was that he wanted to stay because he had made more friends than he ever had. Wow. If adjusting stance and arm placement can do that, imagine the possibilities of really exploring other areas of body language.

Some additional exploration of positive body language led me to the term presence, that is, a presence of confidence, command, and approachability accompanied by a no-nonsense attitude. It is effective in promoting confidence in those who lack it and minimizing overestimated confidence in those who exhibit it.

Presence is also what Dr. Amy Cuddy, celebrated social psychologist, former Harvard Business School professor, and body language expert, wrote about in her book, a New

York Times Best Seller, simply titled *Presence. Presence* is a guide to improving self-confidence through body language and posture and its relation to communication.

By accessing our personal power, we can achieve "presence," the state in which we stop worrying about the impression we're making on others and instead adjust the impression we've been making on ourselves. As Dr. Cuddy's book reveals, we don't need to embark on a grand spiritual quest or complete an inner transformation to harness the power of presence. Instead, we need to nudge ourselves, moment by moment, by tweaking our body language, behavior, and mindset in our day-to-day lives.[16]

Presence is also what Cesar Millan, host of the television show *Dog Whisperer,* uses to mitigate canine chaos, to establish order. He attributes his knowledge of presence to a childhood experience with one of his teachers. At any time, this teacher could enter a room full of rowdy kids and get everyone to be calm and behave. Cesar Millan described how this teacher knew that *presence* was paramount to control. On the surface, it was perceived as rules and strictness, but it in fact was not that. Subconsciously, it was *presence.*

Though *presence* is primarily an informal, unconscious sense of ease, confidence, and self-assurance, it is possible to achieve some consciousness of it through awareness. Presence is about authority, trust, and respect, and it encompasses character, competence, confidence, and a cohesive component—as I call it, compassion. Even police officers, emergency responders, and the military train for what is known as "command presence." It is paramount to their effectiveness to show personal demeanor that conveys leadership and authority but also engenders respect and trust.

Becoming aware that *presence* is an extension of body language and matters in communication is noteworthy, or so I have determined. It is a factor that changes communication in a significant enough way that I considered it to be an important subject to mention. And taking the time to recognize and appreciate influential people in my life has caused me to reflect on why I value them in the first place. I know now that their presence (being a part of my life) and *presence* (character, competence, confidence, and compassion) were paramount to shaping who I am today. Their ability to help me break out of less productive established patterns just the right amount to create change is commendable, and I am appreciative of that.

Also important to mention is a fundamental insight and research concept developed by the Yale Center for Emotional Intelligence. With Dr. Marc A. Brackett at the forefront, as the founding director, this program, RULER, was developed and is an evidence-based approach to social and emotional learning. Dr. Brackett's work studies the role of emotions and emotional intelligence in learning, decision-making, relationship quality, and mental health.

With Facebook, he has developed a number of products, including social resolution tools to help adults and youth resolve online conflict and the bullying prevention hub to support educators, families, and teens.

In an interview on the topic of the emotions of learning, when Dr. Brackett was asked how emotions affect students' performance in school, he answered,

"The idea that emotions matter and matter a great deal in school, but also in everyday life, is at the core of research and programming at the Yale Center for Emotional Intelligence. RULER is premised on a fundamental insight from research: emotions influence attention, memory, and learning, decision-making, health, and creativity. They influence our ability to form and maintain healthy relationships, they are integral to our physical and mental well-being, and they open opportunities for us to succeed in school, at work, and beyond."[17]

"RULER" is an acronym for five skills to regulate emotion:

1. *Recognizing* emotions in oneself and others

2. *Understanding* the causes and consequences of emotions

3. *Labeling* emotions with subtly different vocabulary

4. *Expressing* emotions in accordance with cultural norms and social context

5. *Regulating* emotions with helpful strategies

Research indicates that these five skills are associated with a wide range of important life outcomes, including greater performance, better relationships, enhanced leadership skills, less anxiety and depression, better conflict-resolution skills, and greater well-being.[18]

Aggressive or passive tendencies can be mitigated by considering the RULER approach to managing emotions. The RULER approach has proven to be a great tool for me in the classroom, at home, and in any professional environment. When used as a guide and checklist, it eventually becomes a foundation for communicating. All its parts are significant and regulating emotions will likely take the most time to hone, but can be an influential part of assisting modifying aggressive or passive tendencies. Starting with the RULER system, using it as a precursor, and gravitating toward the ARK Principle. Its guidance to regulate emotions can be a great scaffold to achieve results with the ARK Principle.

Science in Communication

"Rather than being your thoughts and emotions, be the awareness behind them."

~Eckhart Tolle

My goal is to be brief while introducing the idea of how complex the human brain is, in order to help others embrace the scientific side of emotions. Because the human brain is hardwired to be safe, not to be successful, it is difficult at times to genuinely express feelings in a competent way. Understanding this is of great importance because being open, honest, clear, and composed is the key to walking the *tightrope*, that enables the use of the ARK Principle. I believe all this to be so important when there is a situation that dictates that communications are right and even when better communication is simply something we desire.

Staying calm, confident, and capable in a difficult situation or conversation can be monumental and is paramount to effectiveness. It is my experience that this is the main route to achieving balance. This calls to mind a section in Chapter 1 of Daniel Goleman's *Emotional Intelligence: Why It Can Matter More Than IQ*. This information has helped me understand how the brain must work to have reason supersede the much stronger emotional side. In Chapter 1, the section titled "Our Two Minds," Goleman, who has a Ph.D., taught at Harvard, was senior editor of *Psychology Today*, and is trained in behavioral and brain sciences, tells a story of a friend who was experiencing a difficult divorce, one in which her husband left her for a younger woman.

Months of intense bickering and wrangling ensued over assets and the children. In the end, she discovered that her independence was life-altering and liberating. As her eyes welled up with tears, she explained that she reached a point at which she was content to be on her own. This is also the moment when the rational and emotional minds connect, yet the rational mind was the source for navigating and getting through a turbulent life event [19]

Goleman explains:

"These two fundamentally different ways of knowing interact to construct our mental life. One, the rational mind, is the mode of comprehension we are typically conscious of: more prominent in awareness, thoughtful, able to ponder and reflect. But alongside that there is another system of knowing: impulsive and powerful, if sometimes illogical, the emotional mind. The emotional/rational dichotomy approximates the folk distinction between 'heart' and 'head'; knowing something is right 'in your heart' is a different order of conviction, somehow a deeper kind of certainty, than thinking so with the rational mind. There is a steady gradient in the ratio of rational-to-emotional control over the mind; the more intense the feeling, the more dominant the emotional mind becomes—and the more ineffectual the rational. This is an arrangement that seems to stem from eons of evolutionary advantage to having emotions and intuitions guide our instantaneous response in situations where our lives are in peril—and where pausing to think over what to do could cost us our lives." [20]

Goleman further explains how the "emotional and rational minds operate in tight harmony to guide us through the world" and that "for the most part, there is a balance, where the rational mind vetoes the emotional mind and vice versa."

"However, when passions surge, the equilibrium is tipped. The emotional mind takes over and swamps the rational mind." [21]

In a similar vein, Robert Greene, in his book *The 48 Laws of Power*, discusses these sentiments in the book's preface:

"The most important of skills, and power's crucial foundation, is the ability to master your emotions. Your emotional response to a situation is the single greatest barrier to power, a mistake that will cost you a lot more than any temporary satisfaction you might gain by expressing your feelings. Emotions cloud reason, and if you cannot see the situation clearly, you cannot prepare for and respond to it with any degree of control.

"Patience in all things is your crucial shield. Patience will protect you from making moronic blunders. Like mastering your emotions, patience is a skill—it does not come naturally. But nothing about power is natural; power is more godlike than anything in the natural world. And patience is the supreme virtue of the gods, who have nothing but time. Everything good will happen—the grass will grow again, if you give it time and see several steps into the future. Impatience, on the other hand, only makes you look weak. It is a principal impediment to power." [22]

Evidence indicates that excess emotion interferes with successful communication. In fact, on both sides, the aggressive and passive, these intense emotions, nonverbal or verbal, serve as a disadvantage when communicating. This is the crux of the matter and why it is necessary to be aware of how powerful emotions are but that there is immense potential for them to be equally damaging when left to chance.

chapter 11

Core Examples

Intuitiveness, while important, can present challenges, and it requires thought. In light of that, I will share some more insight.

In the educational arena, ZPD, zone of proximal development, is the zone in which students' learning is optimized, meaning that students learn best when they are challenged, but not too much. This optimized state is between what one can do alone and what one can do with adult guidance or in collaboration with more capable peer influence, and insight into what that is per student is based on standardized testing results. It is useful to consider that this optimized state can, in a sense, be applied to other situations in life. I pinpoint this because I frequently use it to guide me in the direction of balance, for myself, others, and the relationship between the two. Intuitiveness is one of the best tools in the real world, since there are no real tangible indicators, like in education. Because it is beneficial to understand with whom you are communicating, based on age, temperament, capability, ability, and personal and professional affiliation, it is important to determine a comfortable space for it to have optimal results. This is especially useful for preexisting and ongoing relationships. This alone supports intuitiveness, which may or may not be a strength, and even if it is, it improves upon it. The ARK Principle suffices for first-time communications, and if intuitiveness is not a strength, regarding this can prompt and kindle it. If nothing else, it serves to minimize the one-size-fits-all mindset and to acknowledge that communication must be tailored to achieve a desired result. It is my experience that articulating this and implementing it outlines a clearer path for positive engagement.

Understanding that skill, age, and social situations require variations is paramount to implementing the ARK Principle successfully. Who, what, where, and when matter. All that is said and done has to be suitable for the audience, for where the audience is. I hope that some of the examples I have provided, though simple, will serve as a platform to what I envision the ARK Principle *looks like, sounds like, and acts like*. This is an extremely meaningful piece to me. A veteran teacher friend used this to help her students monitor their own behavior and the treatment of others. I found that it is applicable to everyone, and to show mercy, compassion, care, empathy, and respect is an integral piece of the ARK Principle. To demonstrate that, I am sharing examples that I believe demonstrate that.

I remember a time when my younger son was eight. I was a single mom at the time and saved up to buy him a special jacket he wanted. He wore it to school the next day but returned home not wearing it. When I questioned him about it, my son told me he had to take off because his friend did not like the jacket. I instructed my son to tell his friend politely,

"I like you as a friend, but the only person who has to like this jacket is me." I told him to be kind, yet firm. I am happy to say he never had another problem wearing the jacket.

I recall a day at the middle school where I substitute teach. That day I was recruited later in the morning. The teacher across the corridor was watching my class, along with his, until I arrived. When he saw me getting close to the classroom door, he pursued his classroom. By the time I got to the doorway, there was a student standing and walking on top of the desks, from one corner of the room to the other. When he noticed me, I politely said with a firm voice, "Excuse me. What would make you think that is OK? That's dangerous." He turned to me, stopped for a moment, and politely said, "I'm sorry. Yes, ma'am. I understand." I was shocked. My firmness, questioning his judgment in the presence of his peers, was all it took for him to evaluate his actions. He apologized more than once, and he did not show any signs of misbehavior that day or any other day I was in that classroom. My reaction also served to set the tone for the rest of the class period, and as word got around to the other future class periods, it served as a precedent.

A younger friend reached out one day to get help because someone had damaged her car. At the request of the person who hit her, and with my friend's acquiescence, the car repair was to be done without insurance involvement. Shortly after the incident, she and I talked more in-depth about a plan. Because she was trying to be somewhat independent, she informed me she would rent a car, but she needed transportation from the shop. By the time her plan was co-ordinated, it was Thursday. She had already found out that the car repair business was not open past 5:00 p.m. during the week, the shop was closed on weekends, and she was being pressured by the person paying for the repairs to take the vehicle in as soon as possible. After some discussion, I suggested that she not let anyone pressure her. So, I hinted she politely communicate that paying for a rental car for a whole week was not practical, and certainly not over the days that the car was not in repair. I also suggested she take charge, call the person who damaged the car, and explain that she would take the car in as soon as it was possible and convenient for her. And that is exactly what was negotiated. As soon as she took charge, she was more prepared to work on a premise that was convenient for her, for which there was no rebuttal.

This particular example above and others that follow remind me of a story from *The Last Lecture*, by Randy Pausch. Randy was a computer science professor at Carnegie-Mellon who was asked to give his last lecture after being diagnosed with terminal pancreatic cancer. In the university arena, professors are asked to give a "last lecture" as if it really is to be the last. For Randy Pausch, he did not have to imagine it was his last since he had just received his cancer diagnosis and prognosis. The lecture titled "Really Achieving Your Childhood Dreams" was his last, but it was not about dying. It was a message to his children about living dreams and everything Randy had come to believe was important for him while living and for his children to know beyond his existence. I have read this book more than ten times, and it is just as engaging each time I read it. In Chapter 55, titled "All You Have to Do Is Ask," Randy tells a story about his and his dad's last trip to Disney World. Randy's son, Dylan, was four years old at the time and really wanted to sit in the monorail's nose cone with the driver. A seemingly benign comment from Randy's dad about how it would be great if "regular" people could sit there would land Randy, his son Dylan, and Randy's dad right in the nose cone of the monorail. All Randy did was ask. I find it to be true, enough to bring attention to it. And I find that this is such an important concept to keep in mind. Further, when I have used it with the ARK Principle, I experienced much the same as Randy Pausch. It really is enlightening.

Another example of "all you have to do is ask," demonstrating the ARK Principle, is a time when my cousin was on her way to have dinner with me, and she got a message from a friend. Her friend called to tell her that the playdate between their daughters was over and that it was time for my cousin to pick up her daughter. My single-mom cousin called me in tears because she was exhausted from work, was on her way to my house for dinner, and was not in a position to immediately accommodate the pickup request. She asked for guidance on a plan, and I suggested she message back and politely explain that she was just sitting down to dinner but could come pick up her daughter after dinner. The mom responded back with "No problem. No rush." Wow.

It was that easy. All she did was ask. She could never have imagined that outcome. My cousin and I enjoyed a quiet, nice dinner that night.

During the pandemic, and with the airline industry hanging in the distance for a comeback, my and my husband's decision for me to return to full time work was a difficult but necessary one. I did not return to teaching but instead decided to draw on experience I had gained before that career. I had used my professional training as an executive assistant many times prior and loved the work. Before long, I began working for a law firm as an assistant. It was my first experience in a law firm, but both the lead attorney and his counterpart agreed that my skills as an academic professional had promising transferability, not to mention I had received formal, professional training years prior. I had taken extensive measures to quantify the integrity of the law firm to which I applied, and I believed the lead attorney had done the same for me as an employee. It was a short time before I realized I loved the work but not the environment. I had the ARK Principle at my disposal by this time, and I believe I could have survived, but I lacked the will to continue. Within a couple of months, I knew I had an important decision to make. My intuition served as a guide for that. I simply could not see myself continuing to serve in my capacity. Over the period of four months, I found myself dreading my work so much that I was feeling anxiety. I approached my boss one day and politely asked him to meet with me. Because I was well into writing my book by this time, I knew nothing more than to draw on what I believed the ARK Principle to be to make gains in this difficult conversation. I arranged a sit-down, face-to-face conversation, in my office, to which my boss agreed. I simply explained that although I was grateful for the immense opportunity granted to me, it was time for me to consider alternative environments. I was open and honest about my feelings. To my astonishment, he agreed to it all. My boss thanked me profusely for my honesty, paid me for all the vacation I had accrued, and gave me a severance. Needless to say, I was shocked, but I was so fortunate to have the ARK Principle as my guide. It served me well.

One of the most poignant examples of the ARK Principle in a professional arena comes from my husband, who, as I've mentioned, is a professional pilot. It is the most useful, proactive use of the ARK Principle I have to share.

During the pandemic, there were many obstacles to overcome on many different fronts. Those of you who flew during the pandemic—right after the world began to slow down—or fly now have heard, seen, or experienced firsthand what the aviation industry encounters on a daily basis. When my husband returned to flying status, altogether ten months hanging on for dear life and hoping to avoid a furlough, we had frequent discussions about a captain briefing that could potentially mitigate negative behavior on the aircraft he was operating and one that would align with the ARK Principle. We also discussed implementing a brief to passengers that would prevent unwanted incidents. As we contemplated to-gether, and though he never shared his message with me until now, I was confident he would send an inspiring, sensible message that would get results. (I have condensed the whole message for practical purposes, but he also uses some humor to engage the passengers, to make them laugh, and to help them feel safe and at ease.) Further, he does not deliver this message from the cockpit, but rather from the aisle so that all passengers can see him, as a real human, that is. I am happy to say he has not had a single incident with passengers while using this message.

"Good morning/Good afternoon. How's everyone doing? Passengers all the way in the back, give me a wave if you can see me. Welcome aboard xxx Airlines with service to (destination). I'm captain Stapleton on xxx flight (flight number) with (time in flight)."

[He explains the weather and continues on.]

"I am working to get the seat belt sign turned off ASAP so you can move about the cabin to use the lavatory and stretch your legs. However, I highly advise and strongly recommend that while you are in your seat, you keep your seat belt securely fastened even when the seat belt sign is off. I have a wonderful inflight crew, and they are here primarily for your safety first, and your comfort after that. Please pay attention to any instructions they give you. Just so you know, those instructions are coming from three places: 1), me, the captain, 2) the FAA, and 3) the federal government of the US." [It is here that he interjects some humor to lighten the mood and make the passengers further feel comfortable and safe.]

"We appreciate your compliance and guarantee you will appreciate the compliance as well. Just so you know, we are real human beings in the flight deck and cabin. I want to pass along my gratitude and my explicit thanks for patronizing xxx Airlines and for allowing me and my crew to try to bring back the friendly skies. With you, it means nothing. You are why we are here. I will talk to you all at the top of the climb."

Though thought must be given to the ARK Principle strategy, it is useful to consider it an evolutionary process. The process of experimenting and evolving with it will pioneer a new path through the sometimes intricate duty of communication. Delivering a message to whomever, whenever, that is courageous yet sensitive and original, and in which the mind is tensile while doing so, need not be overwhelming. In fact, it is freeing because less than desirable responses that are imagined or anticipated do not necessarily materialize. It takes courage to step into this zone, but it is necessary to explore the fact that the desired response is about only considering and expecting it.

chapter 12

Baseball and the ARK Principle

*"I can accept failure. Everyone fails at
something. But I can't accept not trying."*

~Michael Jordan

I relate to baseball because both my boys played baseball for
all their high school years. And since my boys are nine years
apart, I had not one, but two rounds of high school baseball.
Nine years of it taught me so much, and in tandem, the sport
has taught my boys to be resilient, to value adult mentorship,
camaraderie, teamwork, and mental toughness, and most
importantly, to know that failure is a part of progress; it is
not a final outcome.[23] Both my boys were passionate about
baseball, and their efforts and records while playing indicated
that. I believe this sport also shaped them into men of courage
and character, simply because of the synergy of the sport and
the team. Neither of my sons' teams accomplished being part
of a championship, but the teams had remarkable leadership
that encouraged and promoted personal development beyond
measure that is evident to this day.

When my younger son was in high school, I read
a book by Matthew Kelly, an author of multiple best-
selling books who has traveled the globe to spread his

message of enduring authenticity and happiness to millions of people in over fifty countries. In his book *Perfectly Yourself: 9 Lessons for Enduring Happiness*, he includes a chapter titled, "Are You Making Progress?" In this chapter, there is a specific section about baseball:

"We live in a culture obsessed with success, and as a result, we unconsciously foster the attitude that it is not okay to fail. We often measure a person's value by his or her success. Of course, this judgment turns on us when we fail, and we tend to take it personally. If you fail, you aren't a failure.

"I think baseball teaches us more about failure than any other sport does. A great hitter has a batting average of perhaps .350. What does that tell us? It tells us that players succeed in hitting the ball only 35 percent of the time. What else does it tell us? It tells us that he fails 65 percent of the time."

"Francis T. Vincent, Jr., while commissioner of baseball, made these observations in a speech at Fairfield University:

"Baseball teaches us, or has taught most of us, how to deal with failure.

We learn at a very young age that failure is the norm in baseball and, precisely because we have failed, we hold in high regard those who fail less often, those who hit safely in one out of three chances and become star players. I also find it fascinating that baseball, alone in sport, considers errors to be part of the game, part of its rigorous truth."[24]

As I read the full chapter, and specifically this section on baseball, I deemed it appropriate and meaningful as I developed the ARK Principle. It is relative to some central messages suggested in the ARK Principle.

We must not be overcome with failure, because failures are a part of progress. This is true with life in general and with any important, developing change that takes place. The reality is that it will be challenging to find and try new ways to be successful; it may be awkward and discouraging. Yet it serves as a platform for success in future attempts, from which to build, because it leads to aim and purpose.

If powerful and engaging communication is not a strength, it can be. Using the ARK Principle has increased my propensity for solid communications. I remember failing so many times in my first attempts, yet as I kept trying, I realized I had gotten stronger each time too. As I recall conversations gone bad, ones that I found a stronger, more confident message for once I left them, I also reflected on the failures as a platform from which I built confidence. The failure rate may be high, like it is in baseball, but it is certainly higher without a strategy and aim with that strategy. In fact, I believe that communicating is like baseball, in a way. We will likely fail so much at communicating sensitive messages; however, also like in baseball, failing one of out of three times should be perceived as success. I firmly believe that.

I have one last note on baseball and the "three strikes you're out" principle. At some point, I began relying on this principle as a means to assist with decisiveness when communicating. I will try the same thing three times. If I don't succeed, I try a slightly different approach. At times I find myself "scaffolding" this approach, meaning I use some similar threads (words, body language, and attitude; *sometimes you can adjust just one of these and it can be transformational*) from before, but I infuse new ideas to create change. Sometimes I start from square one. Nonetheless, I find this approach successful in generating change, specifically with my communication and as I honed the ARK Principle. If you require some steerage or a starting point, give this a try.

Happiness

"Happiness is a journey, not a destination."

~Buddha

I have always been intrigued with what equates to happiness in life and how to achieve it, simply because I wanted to understand myself first and why I feel personal happiness is an area of strength for me, despite negative influences from sometimes multiple avenues. Countless times, I have assessed information that would give me an understanding of that. I give credit to the bonds and relationships I have formed with an attitude of empathy plus consideration. Both were made possible with the ARK Principle as the focus. An article by Ann Conkle titled "Serious Research of Happiness" gives some insight, and further, it demonstrates just how important communication and relationships are and their direct correlation to happiness:

"Ed Diener is a happy man. In happiness ratings of over eighty psychologists, he came in first. His new book is called *Happiness,* and his position at the University of Illinois is the Smiley Distinguished Professor of Psychology. Diener has spent decades researching what makes people happy. In the 2008 APS David Myers Lecture on the Science and Craft of Teaching Psychology, Diener shared some of the basic findings of research into well-being and how those findings can be brought to the classroom.

"In the US Declaration of Independence, the pursuit of happiness is protected as a fundamental human right, up there with life and liberty. But exactly what is happiness? How do you get and keep it? Why do some people always seem to be happy and some are never happy. Psychological scientists have uncovered some answers and along the way have even examined whether and why happiness matters. As it turns out, happiness does matter in very important ways.

"So, happiness is good. But, how do we achieve it? Diener identifies five factors that contribute to happiness, but the first and second are pertinent to discuss: 1) strong social relationships and temperament/adaptation [and others].

"Happy people have strong social relationships. In one study conducted by Diener, the happiest of 10 percent of the participants all had strong, supportive relationships. A strong social network didn't guarantee happiness, but it was a requirement to be in the happiest group. Temperament, which appears to have a genetic component according to recent studies, also affects mood. Diener discussed the set point theory of temperament, which states that people have ups and downs in reaction to life events, but that they adapt and return to a set point." [25]

This research gives perspective, and there are countless other studies that point in the direction of social relationships' contribution to happiness and well-being. Though I have always believed this, it was not until I began considering *how* I communicate that I finally realized the logic behind it. A review of relationships within my own circle indicates that communication can present challenges at times. Now I have a valuable tool to confidently move in the right direction with those challenges.

Since temperament also affects happiness, I find it useful to elaborate on the importance of considering it when communicating effectively. Although temperament can be influenced by family, culture, experiences, and environment, there is enough evidence to support that it is rooted biologically. There are also benefits that are associated with giving it thought in communications, since it will most likely be a default or a prevailing mood, also known as consistent behavior that is a natural tendency. Body language and brief interactions typically serve to clarify this. Further interactions typically prove it.

After some additional thought on this subject, I concluded at some point that there are two dominant categories of personality. My observation is that there are people who are more generous, thoughtful, agreeable, selfless, contributory, and altruistic, in spirit and actions; others are charming and charismatic yet less agreeable, thoughtful, and generous, in spirit and actions. I venture to say that I always consider this in my communications equation because it is influential, in relation to self and others. This variation in temperament deserves more thought because it takes more to achieve a balance. If temperaments are opposing in my conversation,

I am more attentive. My proactive approaches, words, phrases, and mannerisms are much firmer, and I engage them more often. They are also more expansive. If neither is noticeable, meaning the relationship is reciprocal in temperament, I start with the ARK Principle proactive approach as my default.

chapter 14

Final Thoughts

Communication is a means to connect and at times it is a complex dance. It took a more mature look at my life to fully recognize that. I remember something changed inside me that created change around me. I began to view communication as one of my most valuable instruments for fulfillment and effectiveness, but I understood I had, and continue to have, so much work to do. This more forward way of viewing communication has gotten me closer to accessing resources that have been, and will continue to become, lifechanging. I have learned that the symphony of verbal and nonverbal cues used to convey a message can be played well or not. Considering the instruments used is key to how the "music" sounds. Understanding and using the instruments effectively determines a well-played symphony.

Global shifts with communication as a result of social media influence and the pandemic are palpable and real. Because so much of life is determined by fluency in relationships and communication, my challenge to anyone willing to take control is to consider a specific strategy with which to communicate. It is my personal experience that this is possible through using the ARK Principle and considering the four domains of emotional intelligence: self-awareness, self-management, social awareness, and relationship management. These skills are developed individually, but everyone around us will orient themselves once they see how comfortable and suitable these skills are when explored and honed. From there, the influence broadens.

There is freedom that comes from being open to implementing essential instruments and exploring with possibilities, but it takes a conscious effort. Reining in those possibilities, exploring with them, and carefully developing them, in reference to the ARK Principle, can increase the likelihood of more precise, deliberate communication that emphasizes harmony and balance. Seek options and alternative ways to express thoughts to practice independence *and* personal responsibility. In disagreements, be firm yet polite, and express thoughts effectively. Consider integrity. Circumventing our commitment to improved communication is a detriment to self and to those who depend on us. Stay calm, committed, focused, and fearless in the pursuit of improvement. This is the ARK Principle in action.

chapter 15

The Four Square Strategy: The "Z" Effect

Following the 4 square approach, in order of steps, creates a "Z," otherwise known as the "Z" Effect.

Step 1: Calm (and Composed): First, remember that remaining calm will create a circle of safety for meaningful communication. Once you are calm, there is a platform for engaging in healthy, sensible problem solving and decision making.	**Step 2:** Committed: Second, mentally become attached to the idea that being committed to the cause of powerful communication is of immeasurable positive value. Staying committed to that and acting on it is necessary to communicate effectively and with intention. It is also the commitment to everyone you know that you are investing time, energy, and strength to make a difference. This is powerful!
Step 3: Focused: Focus on not deviating from being calm and committed. Focus on the facts that matter and a positive attitude that will drive momentum and will therefore create a platform for communication that will take place with more ease and fluidity.	**Step 4:** Fearless: Make it happen. Be relentless. Become fearless in the pursuit of improved communication with the ARK Principle. Be fearless with the commitment and fearless in continuing to discover words, phrases, and body language that communicate to others that speaking with intention preserves human beings and the relationships in which they are associated.

notes

1. Gladwell, M. (2008). *Outliers: The Story of Success.* Penguin UK.10. Goleman, D. (1995). *Emotional Intelligence.* Bantam, p. 79.

2. Gladwell, M. (2008). *Outliers: The Story of Success.* Penguin UK.10. Goleman, D. (1995). *Emotional Intelligence.* Bantam, p. 101.

3. Goleman, D., & Goleman. (1995). *Emotional intelligence.* Bantam, p. 42.

4. Goleman, D., & Goleman. (1995). *Emotional intelligence.* Bantam, p. xiv.

5. Gatchpazian, A. (2023). *Assertive Communication: Definition, Examples, & Techniques.* Retrieved from https://www.berkeleywellbeing.com/assertive-communication.html

6. Amen, Daniel G. 2008. *Magnificent Mind at Any Age.* New York: Harmony Books, pp. 233-234.

7. Amen, Daniel G. 2008. *Magnificent Mind at Any Age.* New York: Harmony Books,p. 234.

8. Amen, Daniel G. 2008. *Magnificent Mind at Any Age.* New York: Harmony Books, pp. 253-255.

9. "Respectful Communication." https://www. Respectfulcommunicationandrelationships.Com/Respectful-communication. December 2, 2022. https://www.respectfulcommunicationandrelationships.com/respectful-communication.

10. The Science of Kindness: 101. (n.d.). Retrieved from https://www.psychologytoday.com/us/blog/the-science-kindness/201901/the-science-kindness-101

11. Gatchpazian, A. (2023). *Assertive Communication: Definition, Examples, & Techniques*. Retrieved from https://www.berkeleywellbeing.com/assertive-communication.html

12. Editor, U. (2021, June 17). 10 Positive Body Language Techniques to Help you Succeed. Retrieved from https://blog.udemy.com/positive-body-language/

13. Editor, U. (2021, June 17). 10 Positive Body Language Techniques to Help you Succeed. Retrieved from https://blog.udemy.com/positive-body-language/

14. "Body Language: The Key to Your Subconscious, by Ann Washburn." Video, Editor, U. (2021, June 17). 10 Positive Body Language Techniques to Help you Succeed. Retrieved from https://blog.udemy.com/positive-body-language/.

15. "Body Language: The Key to Your Subconscious, by Ann Washburn." Video, Editor, U. (2021, June 17). 10 Positive Body Language Techniques to Help you Succeed. Retrieved from https://blog.udemy.com/positive-body-language/.

16. "About Amy Cuddy." Amycuddy.Com. February 12, 2020. https://www.amycuddy.com/about.

17. Teaching emotional intelligence using the RULER approach | Resilient educator. (2019, February 7). Retrieved from https://resilienteducator.com/classroom-resources/teaching-q-ruler-approach/Respectful Communication. (n.d.). Retrieved from https://www.respectfulcommunicationandrelationships.com/respectful-communication

18. Teaching emotional intelligence using the RULER approach | Resilient educator. (2019, February 7). Retrieved from https://resilienteducator.com/classroom-resources/teaching-q-ruler-approach/Respectful Communication. (n.d.). Retrieved from https://www.respectfulcommunicationandrelationships.com/respectful-communication

19. Goleman, D., & Goleman. (1995). Emotional intelligence. Bantam, p. 8.

20. Goleman, D., & Goleman. (1995). Emotional intelligence. Bantam, p. 8-9.

21. Goleman, D., & Goleman. (1995). Emotional intelligence. Bantam, p. 9.

22. Greene, R. (2000). The 48 Laws of Power. Penguin, p. xix-xxi.

23. Kelly, M. (2006). Perfectly Yourself: 9 Lessons for Enduring Happiness. Beacon Publishing, p. 19.

24. Kelly, M. (2006). Perfectly Yourself: 9 Lessons for Enduring Happiness. Beacon Publishing, p. 19.

25. Conkle, A. (2008, August 1). Serious Research on Happiness. Retrieved from https://www.psychologicalscience.org/observer/serious-research-on-happiness

Milton Keynes UK
Ingram Content Group UK Ltd.
UKHW052019220424
441570UK00008B/203/J